Macbeth

A PRACTICAL GUIDE FOR TEACHING SHAKESPEARE
IN THE MIDDLE GRADE CLASSROOM

Retold by Christine Hood and Lori Cardoza-Starnes

Illustrated by Don O'Connor

Project Director: Mina McMullin

Senior Editor: Christine Hood

Contributing Writer: Alain Chirinian

Cover and Inside Design: Rita Hudson

Cover Illustration: Don O'Connor

GOOD APPLE
A Division of Frank Schaffer Publications
23740 Hawthorne Blvd.
Torrance, CA 90505

Contents

Introduction

If you asked 100 people to name the greatest writer in history, most of them would probably say, *William Shakespeare.* Shakespeare, a cultural icon of the English-speaking world, has been revered throughout history for his extraordinary skill with language; his unforgettable characters; and his wonderful, many-faceted stories. Some people have been led to believe that Shakespeare is difficult to understand or just not relevant to today's world. Unfortunately, many students' first exposure to Shakespeare may be sitting in a classroom passively listening to the teacher lecture or analyzing passages that seem to have no meaning or relevance to their lives. Studying Shakespeare should not be a "passive" experience; rather, it should be exciting, stimulating, and most of all, fun! It is for this reason that this book was created.

When students are drawn into the humanity of Shakespeare's work, they see how it relates to their lives and the world around them. His themes are central to the struggles and triumphs of humankind; his characters highlight the strength, passion, and joy of humanity as well as its darker, more malevolent side. Although the settings in his stories are in faraway times and places, they deal with contemporary topics. Shakespeare wrote of people in the depths of despair, the throes of comic madness, diabolical plotting, scheming, wooing, and "lovemaking." This may sound like the stuff of soap operas, movies, or TV sitcoms, but that is exactly why students will relate to Shakespeare—a writer for all ages.

In order for students to truly enjoy and appreciate Shakespeare, they shouldn't just read his work, but rather, "experience" it. Before beginning a play study, introduce Shakespeare as a person. Where was he born? What do we know about his life? his family? What was England like during Shakespeare's time? Were his plays as popular then as they are today? What was the life of an actor and playwright like in Elizabethan England? Answering these and other questions for students gives them a personal and historical perspective on Shakespeare and the Elizabethan stage, complementing their overall understanding and enjoyment of his plays.

This book contains a simple summary and an edited version of the play *Macbeth*, in which some language has been simplified for easier student understanding. It also provides suggestions for performing the play; a comprehensive vocabulary list; journal/discussion topics; and a myriad of activities that draw students into the plot, characters, and meaning of the story. These activities will help develop children's imaginations; language and critical-thinking skills; and creative expression through writing, dramatic presentation, and art.

If students' first encounter with Shakespeare is a positive one, they will be "turned on" to future experiences. Learning that "old" doesn't necessarily mean "old-fashioned" opens not only Shakespeare's world to students, but also that of other classic writers and artists.

The Life and Times of William Shakespeare

Shakespeare's plays do not reveal much about him as a person. Since the plots are so varied and deal with a myriad of social and political issues, Shakespeare's actual views remain elusive and mysterious.

Shakespeare's birthday is recognized as April 23, 1564. He was born in the small English town of Stratford-upon-Avon. The town's name developed because Stratford was nestled next to the River Avon. Shakespeare's father, John, was a successful Stratford glove maker who dealt in leather goods; and his mother, Mary Arden, came from a wealthy Catholic family.

Not much is known about Shakespeare until his marriage to Anne Hathaway in 1582. He was 18 and she was 26. During their marriage, they had three children—Susanna, born in 1583, and the twins Judith and Hamnet, born in 1585.

From 1585 to 1592, no official records exist on Shakespeare. But by the age of 28, he had moved to London and become an actor with a small company of players. Even as he became a successful playwright, he continued to act in his own and others' plays. Between 1589 and 1594, Shakespeare's first plays, *Henry VI*, *Titus Andronicus*, and *The Comedy of Errors*, were a huge success in the London theatre circuit. Shakespeare soon made a name for himself and attained instant popularity.

London was a very exciting place during Shakespeare's time. Elizabeth I was queen when he began his career. English ships ruled the seas, and English explorers were claiming territories as far away as America and the Far East. Shakespeare incorporated much of the excitement, mystery, and adventure of this time period into his work. Unfortunately, in the early 1590s, the plague in London led to the closing of all the theatres. During this time, Shakespeare began writing poetry, including his famous sonnets. This poetry demonstrates Shakespeare's true artistic skill with verse.

When the theatres reopened around 1594, Shakespeare helped form the acting company known as the Lord Chamberlain's Men. For the next ten years, it was London's most popular acting company. The company also started it's own theater—the Globe—and Shakespeare became the primary shareholder. The Globe became a popular entertainment spot for both commoners and wealthy aristocrats.

Shakespeare's greatest writing occurred between 1599 and 1608. During this time, he wrote such popular plays as *Twelfth Night, Hamlet, Macbeth*, and *Othello*. In 1603, with the succession of James I, Shakespeare's company received a royal patent, and they changed their name to the King's Men. They were then able to perform at the royal court several times a year.

Between 1610 and 1611, Shakespeare retired to his home in Stratford. Here he collaborated with John Fletcher on three more plays—*Henry VIII, The Two Noble Kinsmen*, and *Cardenio*.

In 1616, Shakespeare died at the young age of 52. Records show that he was buried on April 25, so it's assumed he died on April 23, two days earlier. This date has been suspect since it is also his birthday. No one knows how Shakespeare died, so his death remains shrouded in mystery. Over 20 possible causes of death have been speculated, including writer's cramp, too much alcohol, and murder.

Regardless of what brought Shakespeare to his demise, his incredible life left humankind a prolific treasure in his writings. Shakespeare wrote 37 plays, 154 sonnets, and two narrative poems. His plays fall into three categories: histories such as *Richard III* and *Henry V*, tragedies such as *Macbeth* and *Othello*, and comedies such as *Twelfth Night* and *As You Like It*.

Shakespeare's deep understanding of human nature and his incredible talent for making characters realistic and human make his work uniquely great. Most aspects of human nature haven't changed much from Elizabethan England. One may even find something of him- or herself or a friend in one of Shakespeare's characters. Much as they did in Elizabethan England, these plays can still move audiences to tears or make them roar with laughter. It is these timeless qualities that keep Shakespeare at the top of the literary and theatrical world.

The Elizabethan Stage

Theatre was an entirely different experience for the Elizabethans than it is for audiences today. The stage was round, so the audience was highly involved in the performance. Actors sometimes spoke to the audience through soliloquies and asides, and audience members often answered back. Elizabethan theatregoers yelled, laughed, taunted, talked, and ate throughout the performance.

During this period, politicians and clergy were opposed to the theatre, claiming it was a dangerous diversion from religion. So, playhouses were banned in London's city proper and forced out to the suburbs in an area known as Southwark. In this "theatre district," patrons could choose between nine different theatres. Strewn among the theatres were pubs, taverns, and bawdy houses as well as pickpockets and thieves, which only added to the theatre's already bad reputation.

When a play was about to begin, it was announced with a raised flag and a trumpeted fanfare. The flag indicated the theme of that day's play—black for tragedy, white for comedy, and red for history. When patrons entered a theatre for a performance, they placed their admission money in a box (or "box office"). They could sit in the "galleries" on wooden benches, on cushions in front of the stage, on the stage itself (for more money), or stand in back with the crowd. The general "mob scene" of the crowd (known as "groundlings") created quite a spectacle. Since few Elizabethans bathed, the theatres smelled of sweat, beer, and garlic. It's no wonder the groundlings were also referred to as "penny stinkards."

Vendors sold beer, fruit, and nuts, and in the often tumultuous, rowdy atmosphere of a play, these snacks would sometimes be thrown at the actors onstage.

Like all other playhouses, Shakespeare's Globe was under the patronage of a nobleman. This patronage provided protection from the Puritans as well as additional financial backing. Shakespeare's company was originally "attached" to Lord Chamberlain, and later to James I, becoming the most prestigious theatre company in London.

Shakespeare wrote specifically for his stage in the Globe. Often referred to as a "wooden O," the Globe may have had as many as 20 sides to provide its circular appearance. The theatre was open to the outside and could hold close to 3,000 people. The stage consisted of three tiers—"heaven," "earth," and "hell." A trapdoor in the main stage, or "earth," was used to raise and lower actors and props into and out of "hell." A canopy over the stage was painted with golden stars to represent the "heavens." Often, pulleys and ropes lowered or "whisked" actors up to and from "heaven." A hut on top of the canopy housed props for sound effects such as thunder and cannon fire. Audiences hooted and hollered with delight when such special stage and sound effects were used.

Unlike plays and movies today, scenery and props were limited. To let the audience know what time of day it was or what the weather was like, it was described with an actor's words. For example, when Romeo and Juliet awaken in her chamber, we know it is morning when Romeo says, "It was the lark, the herald of the morn . . . Look, love, what envious streaks do lace the severing clouds in yonder east." Actors also wore elaborate, gawdy costumes and makeup, which were considered sinful by the clergy.

During this time, women were not allowed to act on the public stage, so young boys played the female roles. That is one reason why there are so few women characters in Shakespeare's plays. Not being able to rely on "traditional" feminine beauty for his female characters, Shakespeare created those with amazing intelligence and wit.

Theatres put on a great variety of plays every season. In six months, one company might give about 150 performances of 25 to 30 different plays. Given the quick turnover, rehearsal time was extremely short. Actors only had about a week to learn their parts—up to 800 lines a day for leading roles!

Unfortunately, Shakespeare's revered Globe Theatre burned down in 1613 during a performance of *Henry VIII*. A prop cannon exploded and set the theatre aflame. The theatre was eventually rebuilt, but in 1642, the Puritans finally got their way. The English Parliament passed an ordinance shutting down all theatres, and as a result, the Globe was destroyed in 1644.

About *Macbeth*

"An evil man who kills a king is sordid; a good man who does so is tragic."

—Norrie Epstein

Macbeth is the darkest and most morbid of Shakespeare's tragedies. Most of the play takes place in darkness and the theme of darkness permeates throughout. The play opens in the dark of night upon a barren heath with the three "weird" sisters calling eerily for Macbeth. Later on, both Macbeth and Lady Macbeth call upon darkness to hide their desires and their crime. "Let not light see my black and deep desires," Macbeth pleads, while Lady Macbeth calls out, "Come, dark night, so that my keen knife sees not the wound it makes." Yet near the play's end, it is Lady Macbeth who needs a candle, or light, with her at all times. She can no longer live in darkness (secrecy and guilt) and must face the "light" (reality) of her crime. Her only escape is suicide.

The story's darkness not only obscures our vision of action, but also of intent. Some of the first words spoken in the play, "Fair is foul, and foul is fair," deftly cautions us to not believe everything we see, for it could be cloaked in insincerity. In other words, "appearances can be deceiving." Ironically, King Duncan claims, "There's no art to find the mind's construction in the face," speaking of the treasonous thane of Cawdor. Yet he cannot see Macbeth's treachery. Later, the king's sons suspect this deception, and Donalbain wisely warns Malcolm, "Where we are, there's daggers in men's smiles."

These deceptive outward appearances also contribute to the ambiguity of gender roles, which are vague and blurred between Lady Macbeth and her husband. Macbeth clearly feels "unmanned" by his inability to act decisively, while his wife consistently scorns his masculinity. Meanwhile, Lady Macbeth calls on the spirits to take from her her "woman's natural tenderness" and replace it with "direct cruelty," supposedly a more "manly" quality. At times these characters almost seem to "switch roles."

Macbeth is the classic "tragic hero"—a noble man who commits a heinous crime, his one "fatal flaw" being "vaulting ambition." Macbeth is a valiant, honorable man who allows his desires to control him, overtaking his better judgement and conscience. He becomes tragic when he realizes the emptiness of his ambition, for it is "got without content." And by that time, there is no turning back. Fully conscious of impending doom, Macbeth must accept his fate and move forward toward his own destruction.

Macbeth
Summary

The story takes place in 11th-century Scotland under the rule of King Duncan. Scotland has been warring bitterly with Norway. Macbeth and Banquo, two of the king's generals, have fought valiantly, suppressing the Norwegian king and overthrowing the rebellious Macdonwald and the treasonous thane of Cawdor. In their absence, the king revokes the thane of Cawdor's title and bestows it upon the victorious Macbeth to honor his bravery in battle.

❦ ACT ONE ❦

On a dark and dreary night upon a barren heath, three witches hover over a cauldron, creating a spell for the approaching Macbeth. Making their way home from battle, Macbeth and Banquo run across the witches. "All hail, Macbeth!" the witches cry. "All hail, thane of Glamis, thane of Cawdor, and king hereafter!" Upon hearing this, both Macbeth and Banquo are shocked. Macbeth already retains the title of Glamis, but thane of Cawdor? and the throne? The witches then turn to Banquo and tell him that his children will one day rule as kings. Though Macbeth pleads to hear more of the witches' prophesies, they disappear into the darkness. Macbeth is perplexed and also reminded of his past ambitions for the throne.

As Macbeth and Banquo discuss these strange predictions, Ross and Angus, Scottish noblemen from Duncan's court, greet Macbeth and Banquo upon the heath. They bring news from the king of Macbeth's new title, thane of Cawdor. "But the thane of Cawdor lives," Macbeth protests. Angus relates that the thane has been proven a traitor and will be put to death and stripped of his title. Macbeth and Banquo are confounded by the truth of the witches' predictions. Macbeth trembles with eager anticipation as he thinks about one day also gaining the throne.

Upon returning to King Duncan's palace, Banquo and Macbeth learn that the king has pronounced his son, Malcolm, prince of Cumberland, which makes him successor to the throne. The king praises his two generals for their bravery, and promises Banquo he will be honored and rewarded as Macbeth has been. Duncan plans to visit Macbeth at his home at Inverness, and Macbeth's mind turns to thoughts of murder in order to attain the crown and fulfill the witches' prophesy.

Meanwhile at Macbeth's home in Inverness, his wife Lady Macbeth reads a letter from her husband. The letter describes his meeting with the witches and their strange prophesies. Lady Macbeth decides she must help fulfill her husband's ambitions, even if it means taking part in murder. She ponders on Macbeth's nature, thinking he may be "too full of the milk of human kindness" to go through with the evil act. She realizes she must release herself from the binds of womanly tenderness and concentrate on evil thoughts so she can steel herself against any sympathy she might feel for the king. Macbeth arrives and announces that King Duncan follows shortly after. Macbeth and his wife share an immediate mutual understanding about what must be done that night. Lady Macbeth vows the king will never live to see the morning.

Later that afternoon, King Duncan arrives and Lady Macbeth plays the perfect hostess, leading him off to supper. Macbeth broods, torn between his ambitious desires and his fondness for the king. Macbeth knows the king is well-loved and that he trusts and honors him, yet Macbeth's "vaulting ambition" spurs him onward to the deed.

Lady Macbeth finds him as he stands brooding. She notices his reluctance, and persuades him further by challenging his manhood. She scorns him as a coward and claims she will think him more of a man if he follows his ambitious desires. She shares her plan for murder: First, she will drug the king's guards, rendering the king helpless in his sleep. Then Macbeth will steal into the king's chamber and stab him to death. He will leave the daggers next to the guards, making it appear as if they are guilty of the murder. Macbeth finally agrees to the plan.

❧ ACT TWO ❧

Past midnight, Macbeth runs into Banquo and his son Fleance, who are making their way to bed. Banquo tells Macbeth he has been thinking of the weird sisters and their strange predictions. Macbeth shrugs him off and claims he "thinks not of them." After bidding Banquo and Fleance good-night, Macbeth is left alone. Suddenly, a vision of a dagger appears before him. Macbeth notices blood upon the dagger's blade and takes this as a sign that he should kill the king. Intent on his purpose, he moves toward Duncan's chamber.

After Macbeth commits the murder, he meets Lady Macbeth in the courtyard. Excited and nervous, they discuss what has happened. Lady Macbeth notices her husband is still carrying the bloody daggers and scolds him for his carelessness. She takes the daggers from him so she can place them next to the drunken guards. Macbeth is riddled with fear and guilt, and stares at his bloody hands. Lady Macbeth tells him to wash the blood from his hands and go to bed, where she will soon join him.

Knocking sounds at the gate, and the porter lets in Macduff and Lenox, who have come to awaken the king. Macbeth shows Macduff to the king's chamber, and Macduff returns with the horrifying news that the king has been murdered. Macbeth and his wife feign surprise and sorrow. Macbeth, in an effort to "cover up" the crime, kills the guards who supposedly committed the murder. During the chaos, Duncan's sons Malcolm and Donalbain discuss their suspicions of foul play. Malcolm decides to flee to England, and Donalbain to Ireland. They feel their separation will ensure their safety.

Outside Inverness, Ross and Macduff talk of the unnatural murder. They discuss the obvious treachery of the guards, and then, due to their quick flight, the possibility of Malcolm's and Donalbain's involvement. Macduff informs Ross that Macbeth has been scheduled to be crowned king in Scone.

❖ ACT THREE ❖

In the palace at Forres, Banquo reflects on the predictions of the weird sisters and how everything they predicted for Macbeth has come true. He suspects the possibility of Macbeth's involvement in Duncan's murder. At the same time, Macbeth has grown to fear Banquo. The witches' prediction about Banquo's children becoming kings has left Macbeth desperate to retain his grasp on the throne. He cleverly questions Banquo to find out where he will spend his day, and then employs two murderers to follow Banquo and his son Fleance that afternoon, and kill them.

Later that evening, Macbeth gives a feast for all his noblemen at the palace. During the celebration, one of the murderers comes to tell Macbeth that he killed Banquo, but Fleance escaped. Macbeth feels relieved at Banquo's death, but is unnerved that Fleance still lives. Lady Macbeth urges him to return to the feast and mingle with his guests. As he goes to sit down, he sees Banquo's bloody ghost sitting in his seat. Macbeth is terrified and cries out accusingly to the ghost, "Never shake thy gory locks at me! Quit my sight, and let the earth hide thee!" Macbeth's guests sit in amazement at his bizarre behavior. Lady Macbeth tries to explain away her husband's actions as an illness he has had since childhood, and asks her guests to leave.

When they are alone, Lady Macbeth wonders at her husband's delusions and tells him to get some much-needed sleep. She now worries that he will give away their evil secret. Macbeth promises to keep spies at all his noblemen's houses as well as return to the weird sisters to find out more about his future, no matter how grim. He tells his wife that he has already "stepped in blood so far" that there is no going back.

Meanwhile, Lenox discusses Macbeth with another lord. He speculates about how all those in power who were close to Macbeth have died or fled. He fears Donalbain, Malcolm, and Fleance would also be in danger were Macbeth to find them. Lenox relates that Macduff has gone to England to join Malcolm. There he seeks King Edward's aid in rising against Macbeth.

❧ ACT FOUR ❧

The three witches gather around a steaming cauldron as they prepare another spell. Macbeth soon joins them and demands they answer his questions about the future. The witches offer to show him several apparitions to satisfy his needs. The first apparition is an armored head, which warns him to "beware Macduff!" The second apparition appears in the form of a bloody child. "None of woman born shall harm Macbeth!" the child cries. Feeling reassured, Macbeth asks for more. A third apparition appears—a crowned child holding a tree. He tells Macbeth not to fear unless "Birnam wood to high Dunsinane hill should come against him." The witches warn Macbeth against seeking further knowledge, but Macbeth demands to know if Banquo's children will reign in Scotland. Eight kings appear before him, with Banquo following. Macbeth is horrified by the vision, realizing that indeed Banquo's children will be kings, and the witches disappear. Lenox then informs Macbeth that Macduff has fled to England. In a panic, Macbeth secretly plans to attack Macduff's castle and slaughter all who live there, including his wife and children.

Meanwhile in England, Malcolm and Macduff discuss Macbeth's treachery. Malcolm is at first suspicious of Macduff's loyalties, but soon realizes Macduff is his ally. Ross arrives with news of the attack on Macduff's home and the slaughter of his wife and children. Macduff is devastated and vows to join Malcolm and Siward, who has already formed an army to overthrow Macbeth.

❧ ACT FIVE ❧

Back at the castle at Inverness, Lady Macbeth's gentlewoman calls in a doctor to observe the queen's strange sleepwalking episodes. As they watch, Lady Macbeth enters in a trance, carrying a candle. She rubs her hands together vigorously as if trying to wash them. "Out cursed spot! Out, I say!" she cries. "Who would have thought the old man to have had so much blood in him?" The doctor and gentlewoman are astonished at this confession. Before returning to her chamber, Lady Macbeth sighs resignedly, "What's done cannot be undone." Suspecting the worst, the doctor tells the gentlewoman he thinks Lady Macbeth needs prayer more than medicine.

In another part of the castle, Macbeth hears of the great forces rising against him. He calls for his armor and prepares for battle. Macbeth doesn't feel especially threatened, for he finds comfort in the words of the weird sisters. They promised he would not be harmed by any man "of woman born," or unless Birnam wood came to Dunsinane, both of which seem impossible.

Outside the castle in the Birnam wood, Malcolm and his men gather for battle. Malcolm instructs them to cut branches from the trees in order to hide their numbers and fool Macbeth. In this way, they move toward Dunsinane.

Meanwhile, Macbeth is informed that his wife is dead. Crazed with guilt, she has taken her own life. Full of sorrow and regret, Macbeth expounds on the futility of life and how his "achievements" have left him empty-handed. A messenger appears and tells him that Birnam wood is moving toward the castle. Macbeth is astonished and disbelieving, then begins to doubt the words of the weird sisters, whose lies had seemed like truth. Sensing his impending doom, Macbeth goes out to face his foe.

Young Siward, son of the English general, is the first to find Macbeth and challenge him to fight. Macbeth scoffs him, reassured that Siward is "of woman born." Young Siward is quickly slain. Soon after, Macduff finds Macbeth. "Turn, tyrant, turn!" Macduff shouts with his sword raised. Macbeth and Macduff fight furiously. In defiance, Macbeth tells Macduff he has nothing to fear, since Macduff must be born of a woman. Macduff triumphantly claims that he was not "born" of woman, but "from his mother's womb untimely ripped." Macbeth realizes he has been fooled by the witches, and so refuses to continue fighting. Macduff orders him to surrender and be humiliated and scoffed as a monster before the new king. Macbeth refuses to yield and kneel at the feet of King Malcolm. He raises his sword again and vows to fight to the death.

In another part of the field, General Siward grieves over his son's death, and wonders what has happened to the others. As he speaks with Malcolm and Ross, Macduff enters with Macbeth's severed head, which he triumphantly brandishes upon a pole. All hail Malcolm as the new king of Scotland, and Malcolm promises great rewards to those who were loyal and invites them to his coronation at Scone.

CAST OF CHARACTERS

Macbeth General in King Duncan's army

Lady Macbeth Macbeth's wife

Duncan King of Scotland

Malcolm and Donalbain Sons of King Duncan

Banquo General in King Duncan's army

Macduff Thane of Fife, nobleman of Scotland

Lenox, Ross, Menteth, Angus, Cathness Noblemen of Scotland

Fleance Son of Banquo

Siward Earl of Northumberland, General of the English forces

Young Siward Earl of Northumberland's son

Seyton an officer tending to Macbeth

Three witches

Two murderers

A doctor

A porter

Gentlewoman tending to Lady Macbeth

Apparitions: Ghost of Banquo; Armed Head; Bloody Child; Crowned Child with Tree

Lords, officers, soldiers, attendants, servants, and messengers

Macbeth

Setting

The story takes place in 11th-century Scotland. Macbeth and Banquo, two of King Duncan's generals, have been victorious in battle against Macdonwald and the thane of Cawdor, traitors to the throne. Before the two generals return home, King Duncan hears of their bravery and bestows the title of Cawdor on Macbeth. The play begins as Macbeth and Banquo return home in triumph to their king.

❦ ACT ONE ❦

SCENE ONE *An open field. It is late at night; thunder crashes and lightning lights up the sky.*

Enter three witches.

Witch 1 When shall we three meet again, in thunder, lightning, or in rain?

Witch 2 When the hurlyburly's done, when the battle's lost and won.

Witch 3 Before the set of sun.

Witch 1 Where the place?

Witch 2 Upon the heath.

Witch 3 There to meet with Macbeth.

All Fair is foul, and foul is fair; hover through the fog and filthy air.

Witch 3 A drum! A drum! Macbeth doth come!

All The weird sisters, hand in hand, travelers of the sea and land, thus do go about, about. Thrice to thine, and thrice to mine, and thrice again, to make up nine. Peace! The charm's wound up.

Enter Macbeth and Banquo.

Macbeth So foul and fair a day I have not seen.

Banquo What are these, so withered and so wild in their attire, that look not like the inhabitants of the earth? You should be women, yet your beards forbid me to interpret that you are so.

Macbeth Speak, if you can. What are you?

Witch 1 All hail, Macbeth! Hail to thee, thane of Glamis!

Witch 2 All hail, Macbeth! Hail to thee, thane of Cawdor!

Witch 3 All hail, Macbeth! That shall be king hereafter!

Banquo Good sir, why do you start, and seem to fear things that do sound so fair?

Witch 1 Hail!

Witch 2 Hail!

Witch 3 Hail!

Witch 1 (*to Banquo*) Lesser than Macbeth, and greater.

Witch 2 Not so happy, yet much happier.

Witch 3 Thou shall father kings, though thou be none. So, all hail, Macbeth and Banquo!

Macbeth Stay and tell me more. I know I am thane of Glamis; but how of Cawdor? The thane of Cawdor lives. And to be king is beyond belief; as improbable as being thane of Cawdor. Say from where you get this strange intelligence. Speak, I charge you.

The witches vanish.

Banquo Whither are they vanished?

Macbeth Into the air. I wish they had stayed. Banquo, your children shall be kings!

Enter Ross and Angus.

Ross The king has happily received the news of thy success, Macbeth.

Angus We are sent to give thee thanks from our king.

Ross And he bade me call thee thane of Cawdor.

Banquo What? Can the witches speak true?

Macbeth The thane of Cawdor lives. Why do you dress me in borrowed robes?

Angus The thane lives yet, but his treasons, confessed and proved, have overthrown him.

Macbeth (*aside*) Glamis, and thane of Cawdor; the greatest is yet to come. (*to Banquo*) Do you not hope your children shall be kings, when those who gave the thane of Cawdor to me promised no less to your children?

Banquo But it is strange. And oftentimes, to bring us harm, the instruments of darkness tell us truths; they win us with honest trifles, only to betray us in the end. (*to Ross and Angus*) Cousins, a word, please.

Macbeth (*aside*) If chance will have me king, why, chance may crown me without my help.

Banquo Worthy Macbeth, we stay upon your leisure.

Macbeth Forgive me. My dull brain was wrought with things forgotten.

....

SCENE TWO *A room in King Duncan's palace at Forres.*

....

Enter Duncan, Malcolm, Donalbain, Lenox, and attendants.

Duncan Is the execution done on Cawdor? Have my generals returned from battle?

Malcolm They are not back yet; but I have spoken with one who saw Cawdor die. He begged your highness' pardon, and proclaimed a deep repentance.

Duncan There's no art to find the mind's construction in the face. He was a gentleman on whom I built an absolute trust.

Enter Macbeth, Banquo, Ross, and Angus.

Duncan My loyal generals, you deserve more than I can ever pay.

Macbeth The service and the loyalty I give, in doing it, pays itself.

Duncan I've chosen my eldest, Malcolm, as my successor, and named him prince of Cumberland. From hence to Inverness, and bind us further to you.

Macbeth I'll go ahead, and make my wife joyful with news of your approach; so, humbly take my leave.

Duncan My worthy Cawdor!

Macbeth (*aside*) The prince of Cumberland! That is a step on which I must fall down, or else overleap. For in my way it lies. Stars, hide your fires! Let not light see my black and deep desires.

Exit Macbeth.

Duncan Let us follow him, whose care is gone before to bid us welcome.

SCENE THREE *A room in Macbeth's castle at Inverness.*

Enter Lady Macbeth. She is reading a letter from her husband, telling her of his meeting with the weird sisters and their prediction that he will become king.

Lady Macbeth (*reading*) "This I have thought good to deliver thee, my dearest partner of greatness, that thou might not lose the dues of rejoicing by being ignorant of what greatness is promised thee. Lay it to thy heart, and farewell."

Glamis thou art, and Cawdor; and shall be king as thou art promised. Yet I do fear thy nature. It is too full of the milk of human kindness to catch the quickest path. Thou wouldst be great; art not without ambition, but without the cruelty that should attend it. Come quickly, so that I may pour my spirits into thine ear, and chastise with the valor of my tongue all that impedes thee from the crown, which fate has set before thee.

Enter messenger.

Messenger The king comes here tonight.

Lady Macbeth Thou art mad to say it. Is not thy master with him?

Messenger So please you, it is true. Our thane is coming.

Lady Macbeth Give him tending; he brings great news.

Exit messenger.

Lady Macbeth Come, you spirits that tend on mortal thoughts; take from me my woman's natural tenderness, and fill me, from the crown to the toe, top-full of direct cruelty! Come, dark night, so that my keen knife sees not the wound it makes, nor heaven peep through the blanket of the dark to cry, "Hold! Hold!"

Enter Macbeth.

Lady Macbeth Great Glamis! Worthy Cawdor! Greater than both, by the all-hail hereafter!

Macbeth My dearest love, Duncan comes here tonight.

Lady Macbeth And when does he leave?

Macbeth Tomorrow.

Lady Macbeth O! Never shall the king that morrow see! Your face, my thane, is as a book, where men may read strange matters. Look like the innocent flower, but be the serpent under it. Put this night's great business into my hands.

Macbeth We will speak further on this.

Lady Macbeth It's dangerous to let your face show how you feel. Leave all the rest to me.

....
SCENE FOUR *The same. Before the castle.*
....

Enter Duncan, Malcolm, Donalbain, Banquo, Lenox, Macduff, Ross, Angus, and attendants.

Duncan This castle has a pleasant atmosphere.

Enter Lady Macbeth.

Duncan See, see! Our honored hostess.

Lady Macbeth Here to serve you, your majesty.

Duncan Give me your hand; conduct me to mine host. We love him highly and shall continue our graces toward him. By your leave, hostess.

....
SCENE FIVE *The same. A room in the castle.*
....

Macbeth (*contemplating the murder*) If it were done, when it is done, then it were best done quickly. The king is here in double trust. First, as I am his kinsman and his subject, strong both against the deed; then, as his host, who should against his murderer shut the door, not bear the knife myself. Besides, this Duncan has used his powers so gently, has been so clear in his great office, that his virtues will plead like angels against this sinful murder. Nothing spurs my intent but vaulting ambition, which overleaping itself, can sometimes lead to destruction.

Enter Lady Macbeth.

Macbeth How now! What news?

Lady Macbeth He has almost finished supper. Why have you left the chamber?

Macbeth Has he asked for me?

Lady Macbeth You know he has.

Macbeth We will proceed no further in this business. He has honored me of late.

Lady Macbeth Are you afraid to match your actions to your desires? Would you have that crown which you esteem the ornament of life, and live a coward?

Macbeth I dare do all that becomes a man; he who dares do more is none.

Lady Macbeth When you dared to do it, then you were a man; but, to actually go through with it and become king, you would be so much more the man.

Macbeth If we should fail . . .

Lady Macbeth We fail! But screw your courage to the sticking-place, and we'll not fail. When Duncan is asleep, his two guards will I with wine make drunk. When in swinish sleep their drenched natures lie, as in a death, what cannot you and I perform upon the unguarded Duncan? What can't we blame on his drunken officers, who shall bear the guilt of our great murder?

Macbeth I am settled, and devote all my energy to this terrible feat. Away, and put on your fairest show. False face must hide what the false heart doth know.

⚜ ACT TWO ⚜

SCENE ONE *The same. A court within the castle.*

Enter Banquo, and Fleance with a torch.

Banquo How goes the night, boy?

Fleance The moon is down; I have not heard the clock.

Banquo And she goes down at twelve.

Fleance I take it, it is later, sir.

Enter Macbeth, and a servant with a torch.

Fleance Who's there?

Macbeth A friend.

Banquo What, sir! Not yet at rest? The king's a-bed. I dreamt last night of the three weird sisters. To you they have shown some truth.

Macbeth I think not of them. Yet, when we can entreat an hour, we will have words about that business. Good-night!

Banquo Thanks, sir. And the same to you.

Exit Banquo and Fleance.

Macbeth (*to servant*) Go, bid thy mistress, when my drink is ready, to strike upon the bell. Get thee to bed.

Exit servant. Macbeth sits thinking, then looks up, startled. He sees the vision of a dagger floating before him.

Macbeth Is this a dagger which I see before me, the handle toward my hand? Come, let me clutch thee. (*He reaches out.*) I have thee not, and yet I see thee still! Art thou but a dagger of the mind, a false creation? And such an instrument I was to use. I see thee still! And on thy blade, clots of blood, which was not so before. While I threaten, he lives. Too many words cool the heat of action. (*A bell rings.*) I go, and it is done. The bell invites me. Hear it not, Duncan; for it is a knell that summons thee to heaven or to hell.

SCENE TWO *The same. A room in the castle.*

Enter Lady Macbeth.

Lady Macbeth That which has made them drunk has made me bold. What has quenched them has given me fire. Hark! Peace! It was the owl that shrieked which gives the sternest good-night. I have drugged their drinks and laid their daggers ready. Had the king not resembled my father as he slept, I had done it myself.—My husband!

Enter Macbeth holding the bloody daggers.

Macbeth I have done the deed. Did thou not hear a noise?

Lady Macbeth I heard the owl scream and the crickets cry. Did you not speak?

Macbeth When?

Lady Macbeth Now.

Macbeth Who lies in the second chamber?

Lady Macbeth Donalbain.

Macbeth This is a sorry sight.

Lady Macbeth A foolish thought to say a sorry sight.

Macbeth One laughed in his sleep, and one cried, "Murder!" so that they did wake each other. I heard them. One cried, "God bless us!," and "Amen" the other. Why could I not pronounce "Amen"? I had most need of blessing, and "Amen" stuck in my throat.

Lady Macbeth These deeds must not be thought after these ways. It will make us mad.

Macbeth Methought I heard a voice cry, "Sleep no more! Macbeth murders sleep."

Lady Macbeth Who was it that cried? You weaken your noble strength to think so much on these things. Go, get some water, and wash this filthy witness from your hands.

Lady Macbeth takes the bloody daggers from him and exits. There is knocking within.

Macbeth Whence is that knocking? How is it with me when every noise frightens me? (*He holds his hands up in front of his face.*) What hands are here? Will all great Neptune's ocean wash this blood clean from my hand? No, my hand will rather make the green ocean red!

Re-enter Lady Macbeth.

Lady Macbeth My hands are the same color as yours, but I shame to wear a heart so white. (*Knocking is heard again.*) Retire we to our chamber. A little water clears us of this deed. How easy it is then!

....

SCENE THREE *The same. There is knocking within.*

....

Enter a porter.

Porter Here's a knocking, indeed! Knock, knock, knock. Who's there?

The porter opens the gate. Enter Macduff and Lenox.

Macduff Is thy master awake?

Enter Macbeth.

Macduff Our knocking has awakened him. Here he comes.

Lenox Good morrow, sir.

Macbeth Good morrow, both.

Macduff Is the king awake, worthy thane?

Macbeth Not yet.

Macduff He did command me to call early on him.

Macbeth I'll bring you to him. Here is the door.

Macduff I'll awaken him, for it is my service.

Exit Macduff.

Lenox Goes the king hence today?

Macbeth He does.

Lenox The night has been unruly. Lamentings heard in the air; strange screams of death, and prophesying with accents terrible of confused events. Some say, the earth was feverous and did shake.

Macbeth It was a rough night.

Re-enter Macduff.

Macduff O horror! Horror! Horror!

Macbeth, Lenox What's the matter?

Macduff The king is dead! He's been murdered in his sleep!

Lenox Mean you his majesty?

Macduff Approach the chamber, and go see for yourselves!

Exit Macbeth and Lenox.

Macduff Awake! Awake! Ring the alarm bell! Murder and treason! Banquo and Donalbain! Malcolm! Awake!

The alarm bell rings. Enter Lady Macbeth.

Lady Macbeth What's the business, that such a hideous trumpet wakes the sleepers of this house? Speak!

Macduff O gentle lady, it is not for a woman's ears.

Enter Banquo, Macbeth, Lenox, Malcolm, and Donalbain.

Donalbain What is amiss?

Macbeth You are, and do not know it.

Macduff Your father has been murdered.

Malcolm By whom?

Lenox Those of his chamber have done it. Their hands and faces were all covered with blood. So were their daggers, which, unwiped, we found upon their pillows.

Macbeth O! I do repent that in my fury, I did kill them. Who could refrain, that had loved the king as I did?

Lady Macbeth O, help me! (*She faints.*)

Banquo Look to the lady.

Lady Macbeth is carried out.

Banquo Let us meet and question this most bloody piece of work to know it further.

Exit all but Malcolm and Donalbain.

Malcolm What will you do? Let's not consort with them. To feign sorrow is easy for a false man. I'll to England.

Donalbain And I, to Ireland. Our separation shall keep us both the safer. Where we are, there's daggers in men's smiles.

⚜ ACT THREE ⚜

SCENE ONE *A room in the palace at Forres. Since the king is dead and both his sons have run away, Macbeth has been crowned king of Scotland.*

Enter Banquo.

Banquo Thou hast it all now—king, Cawdor, Glamis, all, as the weird sisters promised; and, I fear, thou played most foully for it.

Enter Macbeth as king, with lords and attendants.

Macbeth Tonight we hold an important supper, sir. I request your presence there. Ride you this afternoon?

Banquo Yes, my good lord.

Macbeth Is it far you ride?

Banquo As far, my lord, as will fill up the time between now and supper.

Macbeth Well, fail not our feast.

Banquo My lord, I will not.

Macbeth We hear our bloody cousins are hiding in England and in Ireland, not confessing their cruel parricide. But we'll speak of that tomorrow. Hie to your horse. Does Fleance go with you?

Banquo Yes, my lord.

Macbeth I wish your horses swift and sure of foot; and so I do commend you to their backs. Farewell.

Exit Banquo.

Macbeth Our fears in Banquo stick deep. There is none but he I fear. He disbelieved the sisters when first they put the name of king upon me, and bade them speak to him; then, prophet-like, they hailed him father to a line of kings. Upon my head they placed a fruitless crown. To make them kings, the sons of Banquo kings! Rather than that, come fate, and I will challenge thee!—Who's there?

Enter attendant with two murderers.

Macbeth Well then, have you considered my speeches? Know that it was Banquo in times past who made your lives miserable. You thought it had been me. This I told you in our last meeting.

Murderer 1 You made it known to us.

Macbeth Both of you know now that Banquo is your enemy.

Murderer 2 True, my lord.

Macbeth So is he mine. And every minute he stays alive tortures my heart. Though I could with my given power have him killed, there are certain friends of both his and mine whose loyalties I must keep. And so I ask your assistance in the deed to mask the business from the common eye.

Murderer 1 We shall, my lord, perform what you command us.

Macbeth It must be done tonight, and leave no botches in the work. Fleance, his son that keeps him company, must die as well in that dark hour. Resolve yourselves; I'll come to you anon.

Murderer 2 We are resolved, my lord.

Exit murderers.

Macbeth It is concluded. Banquo, thy soul's flight, if it finds heaven, must find it out tonight.

SCENE TWO *The same. Another room in the palace.*

Enter Lady Macbeth.

Lady Macbeth Nothing's had and all is spent, where our desire is achieved without content. It is better to be that which we destroy, than by destruction live in doubtful joy.

Enter Macbeth.

Lady Macbeth How now, my lord? Why do you keep alone with sorry fancies your only companions? These thoughts should indeed have died with those you think on. What's done is done.

Macbeth O! Full of scorpions is my mind, dear wife! You know that Banquo and his Fleance live.

Lady Macbeth But their lives are not eternal.

Macbeth There's comfort yet; they are assailable. Then thou would be happy. There shall be done a dreadful deed.

Lady Macbeth What's to be done?

Macbeth Be innocent of the knowledge, dearest one, till thou applaud the deed. Thou marvel'st at my words. But hold thee still; things bad begun are made stronger by ill. So prithee, go with me.

SCENE THREE *A room in the palace. A banquet is prepared.*

Enter Macbeth, Lady Macbeth, Ross, Lenox, lords, and attendants.

Macbeth Sit down and enjoy yourselves. A most hearty welcome!

Lords Thanks to your majesty.

Enter first murderer at the door.

Lady Macbeth (*to Macbeth*) Pronounce it for me, sir, to all our friends. For my heart speaks, they are welcome.

Macbeth See, they embrace thee with their hearts' thanks. (*He turns to the murderer and pulls him aside.*) There's blood upon thy face.

Murderer It is Banquo's then.

Macbeth Is he dead?

Murderer My lord, he has been killed. That I did for him.

Macbeth Thou art the best of the cut-throats.

Murderer Most royal sir, Fleance escaped.

Macbeth Then comes my fit again! I had else been perfect. But Banquo's safe?

Murderer Ay, my good lord, safe in the ditch in which he bides.

Macbeth Thanks for that. Get thee gone; tomorrow we'll meet again.

Exit murderer.

Lady Macbeth My royal lord, you do not give good cheer. The feast is getting cold.

Lenox May it please your highness to sit?

Enter the Ghost of Banquo, who sits in Macbeth's chair.

Macbeth Under our roof would all the noblest be were the graced person of Banquo present. I hope he has only forgotten and hasn't met with mischance.

Ross His absence, sir, breaks his promise. Please it your highness to grace us with your royal company?

Macbeth The table is full.

Lenox Here is a place reserved, sir.

Macbeth Where?

Lenox (*pointing to Macbeth's chair*) Here, my good lord. What is it that moves your highness?

Macbeth (*seeing the Ghost, and pointing*) Which of you have done this?

Lords What, my good lord?

Macbeth (*to Ghost*) Thou cannot say I did it; never shake thy gory locks at me!

Ross Gentlemen, rise. His highness is not well.

Lady Macbeth Sit, worthy friends. My lord is often thus, and has been from his youth. Pray you, sit down. The fit is momentary. Upon a thought, he will be well again. (*to Macbeth*) Are you a man?

Macbeth Ay, and a bold one who dares look on that which might appall the devil.

Lady Macbeth This is just your imagined fear. This is like the air-drawn dagger, which, you said, led you to Duncan. Why do you make such faces? You look but on a stool.

Macbeth Prithee, see there! Behold! Look! (*to Ghost*) How say you? Why, what care I? If thou can nod, speak too!

The Ghost disappears.

Lady Macbeth What! Art thou unmanned by foolishness?

Macbeth If I stand here, I saw him.

Lady Macbeth Fie! For shame!

Macbeth The time has been, that, when the brains were out, the man would die, and there an end. But now, they rise again.

Lady Macbeth My worthy lord, your noble friends do miss you.

Macbeth I do forget.—(*to guests*) Do not muse at me, my most worthy friends. I have a strange infirmity, which is nothing to those who know me. Give me some wine; fill full. I drink to the general joy of the whole table, and to our dear friend Banquo, whom we miss. I wish he were here. To all, and him, we drink; and all to all.

Lords Our duties and the pledge.

Re-enter Ghost.

Macbeth Go from here and quit my sight! Let the earth hide thee!

Lady Macbeth (*to guests*) Think of this, good friends, but as a thing of custom. It is no other; only it spoils the pleasure of our feast.

Macbeth Hence, horrible shadow! Unreal mockery, hence! (*The Ghost disappears.*) Now that he is gone, I am a man again.— (*to guests*) Pray you, sit still.

Lady Macbeth You have displaced the mirth and broke the good meeting with most outrageous disorder.

Macbeth How can you behold such sights and still keep the natural ruby of your cheeks, when mine is blanched with fear?

Ross What sights, my lord?

Lady Macbeth (*to guests*) I pray you, speak not. He grows worse and worse. Questions enrage him. Please go at once; good-night.

Lenox Good-night, and better health attend his majesty.

Exit lords and attendants.

Macbeth It will have blood, they say; blood will have blood. I will go tomorrow to the weird sisters. More shall they speak; for I need to know the worst. I am in blood stepped in so far, that should I wade no more, returning were as tedious as going on.

Lady Macbeth You lack sleep, my lord.

Macbeth What time of night is it?

Lady Macbeth Almost at odds with morning.

Macbeth How say you, that Macduff denies his invitation to our feast?

Lady Macbeth Did you send for him, sir?

Macbeth I will send for him right away! Come, we'll to sleep. My strange visions come from inexperience. We have only yet begun.

SCENE FOUR *The same. Another room in the palace.*

Enter Lenox and another lord.

Lenox Because he failed his presence at the tyrant's feast, I hear Macduff lives in disgrace. Sir, do you know where he hides himself?

Lord Malcolm, the son of Duncan, lives in the English court. He is received by King Edward with much grace. There Macduff has gone to ask the king to help him enlist Northumberland and warlike Siward; that with their help, we may restore peace to our country and live without fear. And this report has so angered our king, Macbeth, that he prepares for some attempt of war.

Lenox Sent he for Macduff?

Lord He did. But Macduff has refused his summons.

Lenox May a swift blessing soon return to our suffering country.

Lord I'll send my prayers with him.

❖ ACT FOUR ❖

SCENE ONE *A dark cave. In the middle, a boiling cauldron. The three witches are gathered around it. Thunder sounds.*

All Double, double, toil and trouble. Fire burn, and cauldron bubble.

Witch 1 Eye of newt and toe of frog, wool of bat and tongue of dog; adder's fork and blind-worm's sting, lizard's leg and howlet's wing. For a charm of powerful trouble, like a hell-broth boil and bubble.

All Double, double, toil and trouble. Fire burn, and cauldron bubble.

Witch 2 Cool it with a baboon's blood, then the charm is firm and good.

Witch 3 By the pricking of my thumbs, something wicked this way comes.

Knocking sounds.

All Open, locks, whoever knocks.

Enter Macbeth.

Macbeth How now, you secret, dark, and midnight hags! What is it you do?

All A deed without a name.

Macbeth Answer me to what I ask you.

Witch 1 Speak.

Witch 2 Demand.

Witch 3 We'll answer.

Witch 1 Say, if thou would rather hear it from our mouths or from our masters?

Macbeth Call them; let me see them.

All Come high, or low; thyself and purpose deftly show.

Thunder crashes. First apparition appears—an armed head.

Apparition 1 Macbeth! Macbeth! Macbeth! Beware Macduff.

Apparition 1 descends.

Macbeth Whatever thou art, for thy good caution, thanks.

Witch 1 Here's another. More potent than the first.

Thunder crashes. Second apparition appears—a bloody child.

Apparition 2 Macbeth! Macbeth! Macbeth! Be bloody, bold, and resolute. Laugh to scorn the power of man, for none of woman born shall harm Macbeth.

Apparition 2 descends.

Macbeth Then live, Macduff. What need I fear of thee?

Thunder crashes. Third apparition appears—a child crowned, with a tree in his hand.

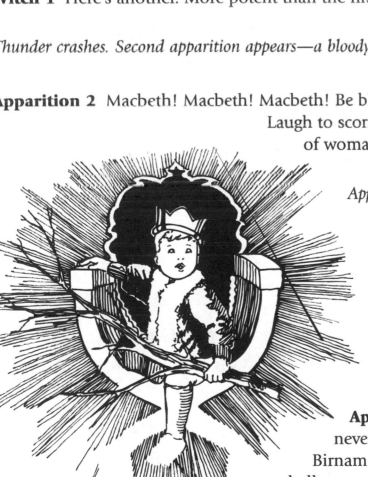

Apparition 3 Macbeth shall never vanquished be, until great Birnam wood to high Dunsinane hill shall come against him.

Apparition 3 descends.

Macbeth That will never be. Who can impress the forest; bid the tree unfix his earth-bound root? Yet my heart throbs to know one thing. Tell me, shall Banquo's children ever reign in this kingdom?

All Seek to know no more.

The cauldron descends.

Macbeth Why sinks that cauldron? And what noise is this?

Witch 1 Show!

Witch 2 Show!

Witch 3 Show!

Eight kings appear, the last with a mirror in his hand; Banquo following.

Macbeth Thou art too like the spirit of Banquo. Down! Thy crown does burn mine eyeballs! Horrible sight! Now, I see it is true. For blood-splattered Banquo smiles upon me and points at them as his. What! Is this so?

Music sounds. The witches dance, and then vanish.

Macbeth Where are they? Gone? Let this wicked hour stand accursed in the calendar!—Come in, from out there!

Enter Lenox.

Lenox What's your grace's will?

Macbeth I heard the galloping of horses. Who was it that came by?

Lenox 'Tis two or three, my lord, that bring you word. Macduff is fled to England.

Macbeth Fled to England?

Lenox Ay, my good lord.

Macbeth (*aside*) Time, thou art steps ahead of my dreadful exploits. And now, I must act upon my thoughts, be it thought and done. The castle of Macduff I will surprise. Seize upon Fife; give to the edge of the sword his wife, his babes, and all unfortunate souls in his line. This deed I'll do before my purpose cools. But no more sights! (*to Lenox*) Where are these gentlemen? Come, bring me where they are.

SCENE TWO *England. A room in King Edward's palace.*

Enter Malcolm and Macduff.

Malcolm Let us seek out some desolate shade, and there weep our sad bosoms empty.

Macduff Let us rather hold fast to our swords, and like good men, protect our down-fallen country.

Malcolm This tyrant, whose name blisters our tongues, was once thought honest.

Macduff From nowhere can come one more cursed in evils to top Macbeth.

Malcolm By many of his tricks has Macbeth tried to win me into his power, but my wisdom forbade hasty decision. I put myself to thy direction. What I am is thine and my poor country's to command. Indeed, before thy approach, old Siward, with ten thousand warlike men, was already setting forth. Now we'll join together, and may our hopes of triumph equal our just cause.

Enter Ross.

Macduff My ever-gentle cousin, welcome hither.

Ross Alas, poor country! Where sighs, groans, and shrieks fill the air unnoticed; and good men die too young, before their time.

Malcolm What is the newest grief?

Macduff How does my wife?

Ross (*to Macduff*) Let not your ears despise my tongue forever, for this shall be the heaviest sound that ever yet they heard.

Macduff Humph! I guess at it.

Ross Your castle is surprised; your wife and babes savagely slaughtered.

Macduff My children too?

Ross Wife, children, servants, all that could be found.

Macduff And I had to be away!

Malcolm Be comforted. Let's make medicines of our great revenge to cure this deadly grief.

Macduff What, all my pretty chickens, and their mother, at one fell swoop?

Malcolm Dispute it like a man.

Macduff I shall do so; but I must also feel it as a man. Sinful Macduff! They were all struck for thee. Not for their own demerits, but for mine, were they slaughtered. Heaven rest them now!

Malcolm Be this the whetstone of your sword. Let grief convert to anger. Blunt not the heart, enrage it.

Macduff O! Bring to me this fiend of Scotland! Set him within my sword's length; if he escapes, heaven forgive him!

Malcolm Come, we go to the king. Our power is ready. Receive what cheer you may; the night is long that never finds the day.

❧ ACT FIVE ❧

SCENE ONE *Dunsinane. A room in the castle.*

Enter a doctor and a waiting gentlewoman.

Doctor I have two nights watched with you, but can perceive no truth in your report. When was it Lady Macbeth last walked?

Gentlewoman Since his majesty went into the field, I have seen her rise from her bed, throw her nightgown upon her, unlock her closet, take forth paper, write upon it, read it, seal it, and return to bed; yet all while in a fast sleep.

Doctor Besides her walking and other actual performances, what have you heard her say?

Gentlewoman That, sir, I cannot tell you.

Enter Lady Macbeth, with a candle.

Gentlewoman Lo, here she comes. This is her habit; and, upon my life, fast asleep. Observe her; stand close.

Doctor How came she by that light?

Gentlewoman Why, it stood by her. She has light by her continually; it is her command.

Doctor You see, her eyes are open.

Gentlewoman Yes, but their senses are shut.

Doctor What is it she does now? Look how she rubs her hands.

Gentlewoman It is an accustomed action with her, to seem thus washing her hands. I have known her to continue in this a quarter of an hour.

Lady Macbeth (*rubbing her hands together*) Yet here's a spot. Out, cursed spot! Yet who would have thought the old man to have had so much blood in him?

Doctor Do you mark that?

Lady Macbeth The thane of Fife had a wife. Where is she now? What, will these hands never be clean?

Gentlewoman She has spoke what she should not, I am sure of that. Heaven knows what she has known.

Lady Macbeth Here's the smell of the blood still. All the perfumes of Arabia will not sweeten this little hand. O! O! O!

Doctor What a sigh is there! The heart is sorely charged.

Lady Macbeth Wash your hands; put on your nightgown. Look not so pale. I tell you yet again, Banquo's buried; he cannot come out of his grave.

Doctor Even so?

Lady Macbeth To bed, to bed. There's knocking at the gate. Come, come, come, give me your hand. What's done cannot be undone. To bed, to bed, to bed.

Exit Lady Macbeth.

Doctor Will she go now to bed?

Gentlewoman Directly.

Doctor Foul whisperings are abroad. Unnatural deeds breed unnatural troubles. She needs the divine more than the physician.

Gentlewoman Good-night, good doctor.

SCENE TWO *A room in the castle at Dunsinane. Outside, the English and Scottish forces join together to attack Macbeth.*

Enter Macbeth, doctor, and attendants.

Macbeth Bring me no more reports. Till Birman wood move to Dunsinane, I will not fear. What's the boy Malcolm? Was he not born of woman? The witches that know all mortal consequences have pronounced: "Fear not, Macbeth; no man that's born of woman shall ever have power over thee."

Enter servant.

Servant There is ten thousand soldiers, sir.

Macbeth What soldiers, fool?

Servant The English force, so please you.

Macbeth Take thy face, hence.

Exit servant.

Macbeth Seyton!

Enter Seyton.

Seyton What is your gracious pleasure?

Macbeth What news more?

Seyton All is confirmed, my lord, which was reported.

Macbeth I'll fight till from my bones my flesh be hacked. Give me my armor. How does your patient, doctor?

Doctor Not so sick, my lord, as she is troubled with fantastic delusions that keep her from her rest.

Macbeth Cure her of that. Can thou not minister to a mind diseased?

Doctor The patient must take care of herself.

Macbeth Throw medicine to the dogs; I'll none of it. If thou could, doctor, find Scotland's disease and return it to pristine health, I would applaud thee. What drug would rid me of these English? Hast thou heard of them?

Doctor Ay, my good lord.

Macbeth I will not be afraid of death and bane, till Birnam forest come to Dunsinane.

SCENE THREE *Country near Dunsinane. A wood is in view.*

Enter, with armor and weapons, Malcolm, old Siward and his son, Macduff, Menteth, Cathness, Angus, Lenox, Ross, and soldiers.

Siward What wood is this before us?

Menteth The wood of Birnam.

Malcolm Let every soldier cut down a branch, and bear it before him. Thereby shall we hide our numbers, and make Macbeth's spies err in report of us.

Soldier It shall be done.

Siward The confident tyrant keeps still in Dunsinane.

Malcolm Many soldiers have given him revolt, and none serve with him but those whose hearts are absent.

Macduff Let us reserve our judgement, and let's to war.

....

SCENE FOUR *Within the castle at Dunsinane.*

....

Enter, with armor and weapons, Macbeth and soldiers.

Macbeth Hang out your banners on the outward walls; the cry is still, "They come!" Were they not enforced with those that should be ours, we might have met them boldly and beat them backward home. (*A cry of women sounds within.*) What is that noise?

Enter Seyton.

Macbeth Wherefore was that cry?

Seyton The queen, my lord, is dead.

Macbeth (*sadly*) She should have died hereafter. To-morrow, and to-morrow, and to-morrow, creeps in this petty pace from day to day, to the last syllable of recorded time. And all our yesterdays have lighted fools the way to dusty death. Out, out, brief candle! Life's but a walking shadow; a poor player, that struts and frets his hour upon the stage, and then is heard no more. It is a tale told by an idiot, full of sound and fury, signifying nothing.

Enter messenger.

Macbeth Thou comest to use thy tongue, so use it quickly.

Messenger As I did stand my watch upon the hill, I looked toward Birnam, and anon, methought, the wood began to move.

Macbeth Liar, and slave!

Messenger Let me endure your wrath if it be not so. Within this three miles you will see the wood coming.

Macbeth If thou speak'st false, upon the next tree shalt thou hang. I doubt those witches, whose lies appear true: "Fear not, till Birnam wood do come to Dunsinane;"—and now a wood comes toward Dunsinane! Ring the alarm bell!

SCENE FIVE *The same. The plain before the castle.*

Enter Macbeth.

Macbeth They have tied me to a stake. I cannot fly, but must stay and fight. What's he, that was not born of woman? Such a one am I to fear, or none.

Enter young Siward.

Young Siward What is thy name?

Macbeth Thou will be afraid to hear it. My name's Macbeth.

Young Siward The devil himself could not pronounce a title more hateful to mine ear.

Macbeth No, nor more fearful.

Young Siward Thou liest, abhorred tyrant. With my sword I'll prove the lie thou speak'st.

They fight, and young Siward is slain.

Macbeth Thou wast born of woman. But swords I smile at, weapons I scorn, brandished by man that's of a woman born.

Enter Macduff.

Macduff Turn, tyrant, turn!

Macbeth Of all men else I have avoided thee. But get thee back, my soul is too much charged with your blood already.

Macduff I have no words; my voice is in my sword.

They fight.

Macbeth Let fall thy blade on vulnerable heads. I bear a charmed life; which must not yield to one of woman born.

Macduff Despair thy charm; and let the devil, whom thou still hast served, tell thee, Macduff was from his mother's womb untimely ripped.

Macbeth Accursed be that tongue that tells me so, for it has cowed my manhood. I'll not fight with thee!

Macduff (*pointing to the ground*) Then yield thee, coward!

Macbeth I will not yield to kiss the ground before young Malcolm's feet! Though Birnam wood be come to Dunsinane, and thou, being of no woman born, I will still conquer thee. Before my body I throw my warlike shield. Lay on, Macduff; and cursed be him that yields first!

Exit Macbeth and Macduff, fighting.

SCENE SIX *The same. Another part of the plain.*

Enter, with armor and weapons, Malcolm, old Siward, Ross, and soldiers.

Malcolm I would the friends we miss were safe arrived. Macduff is missing, and your noble son.

Ross Your son, my lord, has paid a soldier's debt. But he died like a man.

Siward Then he is dead?

Ross Yes, and brought off the field.

Malcolm He's worth more sorrow than I can spend for him.

Siward They say he died well and paid his due. And so, God be with him!

Enter Macduff, with Macbeth's head.

Macduff Hail, king of Scotland! For so thou art. Behold, here stands the usurper's cursed head.

All Hail, king of Scotland!

Malcolm We shall not wait long to bestow our gratitude. My thanes and kinsmen, henceforth be earls; the first that ever Scotland in such an honor named. We must call home our exiled friends abroad, that fled the tyranny of this dead butcher, and this fiend-like queen, who, it is thought, by violent hands took her own life. So thanks to all at once, and to each one, whom we invite to see us crowned at Scone.

VOCABULARY

ACT ONE

ambition desire for power

attire clothing

bade commanded

bestows presents as a gift or honor

bind put under obligation

chamber room

charge command

chastise scold

drenched drunk

esteem value

fair beautiful; pure

feat remarkable achievement or deed

foul offensive; treacherous

heath wasteland

hence from this place

hereafter in the future

hover hang over

hurlyburly commotion; wildness

impedes blocks the progress of

keen sharp

office special duties or position

repentance sorrow and regret for one's actions

spirits intents

spurs urges to action

start startle; alarm

successor one that comes after another in a line

swinish pig-like

thane Scottish title, equivalent of earl

thrice three times

treason betrayal of one's country

trifles things of little importance or value

valor courage; strength

vaulting overleaping; bounding

weird old Anglo-Saxon term for "fate"

whither where; to what place

wrought agitated; excited

ACT TWO

amiss out of place

consort keep company with

entreat pass the time

feign pretend

feverous full of fever

knell funeral bell

lamentings cries of sadness or mourning

prophesying predicting the future

quenched extinguished; eliminated

refrain hold back

repent to feel sorrow and regret for an action

unruly difficult to control

ACT THREE

anon soon; shortly

appall frighten

assailable can be attacked

bides dwells; stays

blanched turned white

botches mistakes

commend deliver

fancies fantasies

fie expression of disgust

fruitless unsuccessful

gory covered with blood

hie hurry

ill evil

infirmity sickness

locks hair

VOCABULARY

marvel wonder at; to be amazed

mirth joy

mischance bad fortune

mockery imitation

muse wonder at; marvel

parricide killing of one's own parent

resolve make a firm decision

tedious tiresome because of extreme slowness

tyrant brutal, oppressive ruler

ACT FOUR

accursed cursed

adder poisonous snake

apparition ghostly figure

blunt dull

convert change

deftly skillfully

demerits offenses; sins

desolate lonely

despise hate

dispute resist; go against

exploits acts; deeds

fiend wicked person

howlet small owl

impress take by force

newt type of lizard

one fell swoop one fierce motion

potent having strong effect or influence

resolute determined; strong

vanquished defeated; conquered

whetstone stone for sharpening tools

ACT FIVE

abhorred causing hate and disgust

abroad in a foreign country

bane murder; destruction

brandished waved in a threatening way

charged burdened

confirmed established with certainty

cowed destroyed the courage of

delusions false beliefs or images

despair lose hope

divine superhuman being or god

endure suffer

err error; mistake

exiled removed forcefully from a country; banished

frets worries

mark notice; pay attention

minister to give aid

mortal of humankind

perceive become aware of

petty insignificant; small-minded

player actor

pristine original

revolt rebellion; renounce allegiance

scorn reject as unworthy

snares traps

untimely before the natural time; prematurely

usurper one who seizes and holds power by force

vulnerable sensitive to attack or harm

wrath vengeful anger

"All the world's a stage, and all the men and women merely players." This quote from Shakespeare's delightful comedy *As You Like It* is a great way to begin your study of Shakespeare. Ask students what they think this quote means. Explain that "players" are actually "actors." Shakespeare meant that throughout our lives, we play many different roles—children, teenagers, and adults; daughters, sons, mothers, fathers, cousins, friends, workers, and so on. We also "act" within our life roles. Play-acting is a part of everyday existence. Ask students when they might "act" in real life. Invite them to act out an incident from their lives for the class (for example, a problem with a sibling, a funny incident with a family member or friend, or an embarrassing moment). Students can have lots of fun with this;

encourage them to be creative, yet true to life.

 Ask students if they have ever seen a stage play. Discuss the difference between acting onstage, in the movies, or on TV. In Shakespeare's time, there were no TVs, movies, radios, or video games, so entertainment usually came in the form of drama. Drama did not begin with Shakespeare. Plays were watched with rapt attention by theatregoers many centuries before him. Drama is thought to have developed from many sources—an outgrowth of religious ceremonies to appease the gods; songs at grave sites or about heroes, extolling their virtues; to preach morals to the masses; and simply to satisfy people's natural love for storytelling and entertainment. Drama was and still is a way to "get away from it all" and have a good time. It creates an

opportunity for us to laugh at ourselves as we see life reflected in the many human characters and situations portrayed before us.

 Showing videotapes of Shakespearean plays helps children understand the nuances of drama, and how Shakespeare's language and characterization bring his stories to life. Many of Shakespeare's plays are available on videotape. Watch a video and/or compare one video interpretation to another. Make sure to view videos before showing them to your class, as some material may be unsuitable due to language or adult situations. However, don't let videos replace the reading and performing of plays by your students. Shakespeare is meant to be experienced as a live performance.

SHAKESPEAREAN TRAGEDY

"[Shakespearean] tragedy is not defined by what it does but by what it does to us. In tragedy we are stripped of the defenses that keep us from looking at life's dark underside . . . and a world of absolutes—mortality, time, death, decay, good, and evil—is revealed."

—Norrie Epstein

 Why is Shakespearean tragedy so ultimately heartbreaking? Because it reflects the weaknesses in all of us. It shows human beings struggling with their existence, only to find destruction at its end.

 Just as in his comedies, Shakespeare's tragedies present their characters with harrowing circumstances, obstacles to overcome, temptations, and difficult choices. But unlike comic characters, tragic characters are unable to effectively deal with these circumstances, cannot overcome obstacles, give in to temptation, and make all the wrong choices. Shakespeare's comic characters are given second and sometimes third chances to deal with their problems, while his tragic characters are thrown headlong into destruction, with no turning back.

 Shakespeare uses tragedy to strip away all the "niceties" we show to the world to uncover what lies beneath—our deepest fears, our longings, and our appetite for those things not always deemed "pleasant" or "acceptable"—revealing our mortal souls and the good and evil in all of us.

 Shakespeare utilizes what Aristotle once called the "tragic hero." The tragic hero is a noble character, lofty in his station, seeming to "have it all." He is not a man of absolutes, but of earthly, human needs and desires. And it is exactly how this character acts on those desires that makes him tragic. For example, had Othello not believed Iago's lies of infidelity about Desdemona, Othello would not have felt compelled to kill her, a woman with whom he was very much in love; if Hamlet had come forth with what he knew about his father's murder, or quickly and decisively killed his uncle instead of lingering in self-doubt, a much different fate may have befallen him. Similarly, if Macbeth had simply contented himself with his new title, and not allowed his "vaulting ambition" to control him, he too, we assume, would have gone on to live a fruitful, successful life.

 These "heroes" aren't completely evil, for if they were, wherein would lie the tragedy? It is the "good" man who loses himself that makes a tragic downfall. It is his wanting to go back and change his deeds or decisions, yet finds he cannot, that constitutes Shakespearean tragedy.

At first, "Shakespearean language" can seem overwhelming to students. Many students have heard Shakespeare quoted, but have no idea what these quotes mean. Though the language may seem complex, it was common in England at the time the plays were written. It's no wonder students may feel overwhelmed reading even an edited version of a Shakespearean play. It's been estimated that he uses between 25,000 and 29,000 different words in his plays and poems! But among all the "thees" and "thous" are many common, everyday expressions students will be amazed to know originated with Shakespeare (or "the bard"). Write several of the following Shakespearean expressions on the board and invite students to guess what they mean. They'll be surprised at how these expressions have endured through time.

Apple of her eye

Bated breath

Budge an inch

Dead as a door nail

Eating me out of house and home

Eyesore

For goodness' sake

The game is up

Good riddance

Green-eyed monster

Household words

Knock, knock, who's there?

Laughingstock

The naked truth

Neither rhyme nor reason

One fell swoop

The primrose path

Such stuff as dreams are made on

Suit the action to the word

Sweets to the sweet

To thine own self be true

Too much of a good thing

Tower of strength

Wear my heart on my sleeve

What's done is done

LET'S PUT ON A PLAY!

 If you decide to produce the play, you can make it as small or as large a production as you like. You may decide on just an "in-class" production, maybe inviting one or two classes to the performance; or you may want to perform for parents or the whole school. Decide which experience would most benefit your students and meet your classroom needs. When deciding the kind of production you want, consider the time you will need to invest and your classroom budget. It's advantageous for students to be able to perform more than once so they can evaluate and discuss areas for improvement.

When deciding the kind of production you want, consider the time you will need to invest and your classroom budget.

 Discuss with students which type of production they prefer. Do they want a "classic" Shakespearean production, or do they want to get creative with their interpretation? Students can modernize the play, set it in a different time and/or place, or they can interject their own vernacular. There are many innovative ways to approach a Shakespearean production, so encourage students to brainstorm how they can make theirs original and interesting. Remind them that the fun of putting on a play is in the *process*, not necessarily the *performance*. Make it simple (props, costumes, scenery) so students will get the most out of the experence.

 Most students will want to act in the play, and there's a good chance that several will want the leading roles. Since one purpose of performing plays is to increase self-esteem and self-confidence, it wouldn't make sense to choose only the most poised, confident students in the class. On the other hand, choosing a cast of shy, introverted actors will lessen the strength of and interest in the play. If possible, try and balance your cast. It's also helpful to choose actors who will help each other develop their parts in the friendly spirit of cooperation. Since there are fewer female than male roles, allow girls to play boys' parts and vice versa. Consider the following questions when choosing actors.

- **Does the student have a voice that carries? If not, can he or she bring up the voice level?**

- **Does the student show imagination and enthusiasm for the part?**

- **Does he or she have "stage presence"?**

- **Can the student think on his or her feet and bring the role to life?**

Auditions can be intimidating and possibly embarrassing for many students. Instead of having them audition for the entire class, invite small student groups to audition different roles for the play. During tryouts, encourage students to offer encouragement and constructive criticism. "Can you look more at the audience?" is obviously better than "He never looks at the audience. He's terrible!" Before tryouts begin, discuss with students how to give constructive criticism in a kind, helpful, and respectful way. Write a list of rules on the board (e.g., *Be positive*; *Critique the "work," not the person*; and so on). As an alternative, invite students to write comments on note cards and give them to you. Read only those comments that are truly "constructive" and helpful to the performing student. Remind students that there is no one "right" way to do Shakespeare. A diversity of characterizations only adds dimension to the production. Invite groups to brainstorm each role and discuss their ideas with auditioning students.

 Even if your class is large, you can still get everyone involved in the production. Many students will want to act in the play, but some may prefer to work "behind the scenes." Emphasize that all jobs are important to a production. Invite interested students to "apply" for the following jobs by writing a short paragraph about why they would be good at a particular task, or you can simply hold "interviews" with individual students. Encourage them to have first and second choices, so everyone has a chance to do something he or she enjoys.

Critique the "work," not the person.

DIRECTOR

You may want to assume this responsibility, using one or two student assistants. The director helps place actors and scenery in the correct places, reminds actors when and how to project their voices, and keeps rehearsals structured. This is a difficult task, so make sure you choose students who aren't too "bossy." Many a production has crumbled because everyone resented the director's bossy ways.

UNDERSTUDIES

Necessary only for the leading roles. If there is more than one performance, they may play the leads the second time.

PROMPTER

Stands offstage during rehearsals and performances, and whispers lines and/or hints for the actors in case they forget their lines or where they should be onstage.

STAGE MANAGER AND ASSISTANT

Ensure that production is going smoothly and all scenery and props are in place.

MAKEUP ARTISTS

Decide on and apply makeup to actors before performances. You may want to have two or three students for this job. Call local cosmetology schools or colleges with theater departments for help.

COSTUMERS

Research the time period in which the play takes place, and create costumes from available materials. (Ask parents to donate old clothes and fabric scraps.) Simple costumes such as tunics can be made from large shirts cinched with belts, and sweatpants can be pulled up to look like Renaissance-period pants.

LET'S PUT ON A PLAY!

LIGHTING SPECIALIST

Works with the director to manipulate lighting for dramatic effects.

CURTAIN SPECIALIST

Raises and lowers the curtain at the appropriate times.

SCENERY AND PROP CREW

Finds and/or makes appropriate scenery and props for the play, sets up and takes down scenery during the performance, and cleans the stage and "theater" after performances.

ADVERTISING AND PUBLICITY CREW

Makes posters advertising the play. If you're inviting the whole school, write ads about the play and have them announced over the school intercom. If your production is going to be large, you might consider advertising it in your local newspaper or on your local public-access channel.

PLAYBILL WRITERS AND ILLUSTRATORS

Design and write a simple playbill with short blurbs about Shakespeare, the play, actors, scenes, and so on. This will add a nice dimension to your production.

TICKET TAKER

Necessary if you have parents coming to the performances. Most school plays are free, but you can "sell" tickets in exchange for a can of food for a local homeless shelter, a can of pet food or supplies for a local animal shelter, or other charitable donations.

USHERS

Show people to their seats and make certain "unruly" students keep quiet during performances.

VIDEOGRAPHER

Videotapes performances. This is great not only for critiquing the play later, but also authenticates the experience for students. They will love watching themselves on television. You may even want to make copies for families and friends to keep!

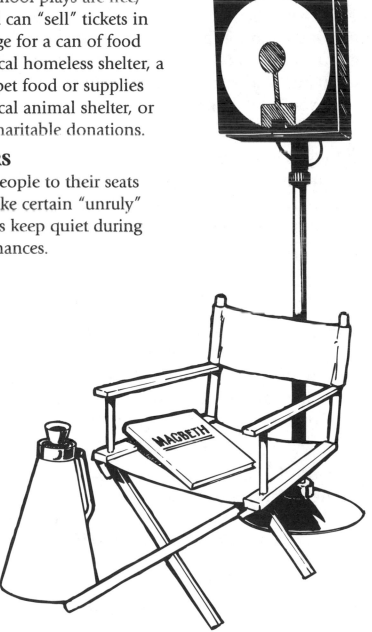

JOURNAL/DISCUSSION TOPICS

To inspire students to think critically and form opinions, offer several of the following journal ideas for discussion, reflection, and writing.

❧ ACT ONE ❧

◈ At the beginning of the play, the three witches chant, "Fair is foul, and foul is fair." Write about something that is ugly, or "foul," on the inside, yet beautiful, or "fair," on the outside. This sounds much like the phrase, "Beauty is only skin deep." What do you think this means? Consider how the phrase applies to Macbeth and his wife. Do they appear "fair" to those around them? Explain.

◈ Macbeth claims to have "vaulting ambition" for the throne. Write about three of the most important ambitions you have for your life, and rank their importance. Think about your number-one ambition. Why is this goal so important? Macbeth went to extreme lengths to achieve his goal. What would you be willing to do to achieve yours?

◈ Lady Macbeth tries her best to convince Macbeth to kill King Duncan. Do you think Macbeth would have gone through with the murder had she not been there to persuade him? Tell about a time someone tried to talk you into doing something you weren't sure about. How did it make you feel? Were you convinced?

❧ ACT TWO ❧

◈ In the play, there are many references to darkness and nighttime. Brainstorm as many things as you can that are dark, then write which ones might be thought of as scary. Write about why you think nighttime seems scarier than daytime. Then comment on why both Macbeth and his wife yearn for the night, or darkness, to fall.

◈ Macduff ironically believes Lady Macbeth faints because she is too delicate a woman to be exposed to Duncan's murder. List all the adjectives describing the stereotype of how a woman is "supposed to be." Then describe how Lady Macbeth goes against that stereotype.

JOURNAL/DISCUSSION TOPICS

Lady Macbeth and her husband must both act surprised and horrified at Duncan's death. Write about a time you had to pretend to feel one way while feeling the opposite. Were you successful? How did it make you feel? Do you think it's dishonest to act one way and actually feel another? Can you think of a particular situation in which it might good idea? Explain.

⋙ ACT THREE ⋘

Lady Macbeth mocks her husband's masculinity when he claims to see Banquo's ghost. List five men you think of as very "masculine" and five women you think of as very "feminine." Describe why you think these are good examples. What do you think makes someone masculine or feminine? Write a short definition for each, and then explain why you think Lady Macbeth makes fun of her husband's "masculinity."

Most people in Shakespeare's day believed in ghosts and witches. Do you believe Banquo's ghost was real or simply Macbeth's guilt playing tricks on him? Write about a ghost story you have heard. Do you believe in ghosts or do you think it is all nonsense?

Lady Macbeth complains that her desire is "achieved without content." What do you think she means by this? Have you ever wanted something badly and then felt disappointed when you actually got it? Describe a time when this happened to you. Why do you think you were disappointed?

⋙ ACT FOUR ⋘

The witches add things such as "eye of newt" and "toe of frog" to their brew. Write a recipe for your own "magic brew." Include ingredients, measurements, and directions. Be creative, and include what magic this brew will perform.

Macbeth believes the witches hold all the answers to his life. If Macbeth would have waited for destiny to come to him instead of acting upon it, do you think he still would have become king? Why or why not? Do you believe your life is already planned out or that you have control over your own destiny? How do circumstances and luck play into our destinies?

⊞ Macduff is overcome with grief at the death of his family. Malcolm consoles him by advising him to let "grief convert to anger" and go after Macbeth. Do you agree with this advice? What advice would you give to Macduff?

⌘ ACT FIVE ⌘

⊞ Some believe that sleep is the privilege of the innocent and honorable. How does this idea play out in Macbeth? Why do you think Lady Macbeth sleepwalks?

⊞ Malcolm and Macduff feel justified in starting a war to overthrow Macbeth and seize the crown for Malcolm. Do you think their war is justified? Explain. List five reasons why a country should go to war, and five reasons why it shouldn't. Compare your list with classmates', and decide which includes the strongest arguments.

⊞ Near the end of the play, Macbeth claims that man is simply "a poor player, that struts and frets his hour upon the stage, and then is heard no more . . . signifying nothing." What do you think he means by this statement? How does this statement reflect the way Macbeth feels about his own life and impending death?

ALL THE WORLD'S A READERS' THEATER

You may wish to perform the play as a readers' theater rather than a full production. This technique allows students to participate with little preparation. You can even assign two or three students to one role. Make sure students have thoroughly reviewed the play and their lines before performing. Even though this will be an informal performance, encourage students to wear costumes and stand or walk around when their characters are speaking.

IMPROMPTU PERFORMANCES

After reading and discussing the summary of the story, divide the class into seven or eight groups and distribute a summary to each. Have groups decide where they think the summary should be broken down into scenes. Depending on your class size, have groups each take responsibility for performing one or two scenes for the class. Invite groups to perform using their own interpretation and language. Students will enjoy using their own "lingo," and you will be amazed to see the play come to life with students' own words and emotions.

Before groups perform, have them write a short summary of the scenes for which they are responsible. For example:

Scene One—The three witches predict Macbeth will be thane of Cawdor and the future king; they predict Banquo will be the father of kings. Ross and Angus tell Macbeth he is now thane of Cawdor, fulfilling one of the witches' predictions.

Scene Two—Macbeth and Banquo return to the palace, and King Duncan praises their victory in battle. Macbeth learns that Malcolm, Duncan's son, will succeed Duncan to the throne.

Scene Three—Lady Macbeth learns of the witches' predictions through a letter from Macbeth. She vows to help her husband get the throne by killing Duncan.

Scene Four—King Duncan arrives at the castle and Lady Macbeth plays the perfect hostess.

Scene Five—Macbeth and his wife discuss a plan for killing the king in his sleep that night. Macbeth has mixed feelings, but decides to go through with the murder anyway.

MACBETH'S CENTRAL THEMES

Reproduce these quotes from *Macbeth*, cut them apart, and distribute them to students. Have students read their quotes aloud several times, and ask them which ideas were repeated. Place signs around the room reading *Darkness, Masculinity vs. Femininity, Sleeplessness, Blood = Guilt,* and *Appearances Can Be Deceiving.* Have students go to the sign that best represents their quotes, and then, as a group, write a poetic phrase by combining their quotes together. This is a great way to introduce as well as review *Macbeth*'s central themes.

- Fair is foul, and foul is fair.
- You should be women, yet your beards forbid me to interpret that you are so.
- Stars, hide your fires! Let not light see my black and deep desires.
- I dare do all that becomes a man.
- Look like the innocent flower, but be the serpent under it.
- Macbeth murders sleep!
- It will have blood, they say; blood will have blood.
- Art thou unmanned by foolishness?
- My soul is too much charged with your blood already.
- There's no art to find the mind's construction in the face.
- This is her habit; and, upon my life, fast asleep.
- Dispute it like a man.
- Out, out, brief candle!
- Where we are, there's daggers in men's smiles.
- Life's but a walking shadow.
- O gentle lady, it is not for a woman's ears.
- False face must hide what the false heart doth know.
- Sleep no more!
- Here's the smell of blood still.
- It has cowed my better part of man.
- I am in blood stepped in so far, that . . . returning were as tedious as going on.
- When shall we three meet again, in thunder, lightning, or in rain?
- Will all great Neptune's ocean wash this blood clean from my hand?
- When was it she last [sleep]walked?
- Come, dark night, so that my keen knife sees not the wound it makes.

REBUILDING THE GLOBE

Invite student groups to construct small versions of the Globe Theatre. They can use boxes, cardboard tubes, tagboard, fabric and wrapping-paper scraps, yarn, and various other art supplies. Make sure they refer to an accurate picture of the Globe and include the many special attributes of Shakespeare's stage, including trapdoors that fall into "hell" and a canopy above the stage as "heaven." Encourage students to be creative and add actors onstage as well as patrons in the audience. Invite students to display their creations. As an extension, invite groups to "act out" a scene from the play using their theatres, and characters made from cardboard, spools, or even sock puppets, depending on the size of the models.

GOOD FORTUNE

Before beginning your play study, have each student choose a fortune out of a hat. All the fortunes should be positive, such as:

You will win the lottery and receive 12 million dollars.

You will become a famous and talented movie star.

You will become president of the United States.

You will recover the first actual alien spacecraft.

You will discover the cure for cancer.

Invite students to read their fortunes aloud to the class. Discuss whose fortunes they'd most like to have and the reasons for their choices. Have students write what steps they would have to take to ensure these prosperous futures, and how far they would be willing to go to achieve them.

After reading and discussing Act One of the play, compare and contrast student responses to Macbeth's. Draw a large Venn diagram on the board and write students' responses in one circle, Macbeth's in the other, and common responses in the middle section.

DEAR DIARY

After studying each act of the play, invite students to each choose a character who appears in that act. Have students write diary entries from the character's perspective, describing how he or she feels and what he or she plans to do. Students will look forward to seeing what their characters actually decide to do in the following act. This helps students look into the minds of the characters, see things from their perspective, and predict what what will happen next in the story.

3-D CHARACTER MASKS

Invite students to each make a 3-D mask of Macbeth or Lady Macbeth. Have students cut a mask shape from construction paper, cutting out eyes and a mouth. Then have them cut a 1" (2.5-cm) slit in the chin, and two 1" (2.5-cm) slits in the forehead over the eyes (see Step 1). Invite them to draw three symbols on their masks representing the qualities their characters show the world (e.g., a lion for *courageous*, a flower for *beautiful*, and a heart for *loving*), and include quotes from the play underneath which "prove" these outward qualities. Have students fold the "tabs" over each other in the back, and staple to create a 3-D effect (see Step 2). On a separate sheet of paper cut to fit the mask's shape, have students draw three symbols representing the character's true inner feelings, motives, and desires, including quotes underneath. Students then attach the paper to the back of their mask so it can be "seen" through the eyes in the front. Invite them to add yarn "hair" and "beards," sequin "jewels," and other decorations (see Step 3). Have students write a short paragraph explaining what their mask represents on the outside and inside. Display masks around the room. As an extension, invite students to compare their masks to one of the play's central themes: "Fair is foul, and foul is fair."

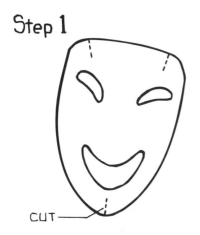

Step 1

CUT

Step 2

BACK OF MASK

FOLD "TABS" AND STAPLE

Step 3

YARN

SEQUINS

MACBETH IN THE TABLOIDS

Show students various funny or outrageous headlines from sensationalist newspapers, and share some of the wild stories that accompany them. Compare these with traditional newspapers and discuss the differences. Ask students which scenes from *Macbeth* would make great tabloid news, and which would be better placed in a traditional newspaper. Invite student groups to choose a good "news story" from the play and create two articles—one for a tabloid and one for a traditional newspaper. For the tabloid, students can write a silly headline, draw a "doctored photo," and write outrageous, sensational copy. What claims can be made? How can the truth be stretched? What sources or leads can be cited? For the traditional newspaper, have students create a headline, photo, and copy, but with a realistic, authentic viewpoint. Afterward, compare and contrast these very different types of writing. For example, how can both types of papers present Macbeth's feast and his claim to see Banquo's ghost? the king's murder? the three witches on the heath, predicting the future?

ALPHABET COUPLETS

Assign student pairs two concurrent letters of the alphabet. Invite them to write and illustrate an alphabet couplet reviewing any theme, character, or prop in the play. When they are finished, display the couplets around the room for an instant play review! For example:

A is for ambition,
Macbeth kills to be great.

B is for Banquo,
His sons kings, it is fate!

C is for cauldron,
Spells boiled in a pot.

D is for Duncan,
In Macbeth's trap he is caught.

CHARACTER COLLAGE

Divide students into groups of four or five, and give each a large sheet of butcher paper. Have one student lie on the paper, and another trace around his or her body with black marker. The tracing will represent Macbeth or Lady Macbeth. Invite students to use symbols, cutouts, drawings, quotes, and so on to fill their characters. The mouth can contain quotations; the eyes, visions—imaginary or real; the hands, actions; the heart, emotions; the stomach (gut), fears; and the legs and feet, movement and journeys. Have groups write about what their symbols mean and then present their collages to the class.

MONOLOGUE PICTURE SCROLLS

This activity can be done after each monologue that may be difficult for students to understand, yet is ripe with symbolism. Examples include *Act One, Scene Three: Lady Macbeth schemes after reading the letter from Macbeth; Act One, Scene Five: Macbeth contemplates killing the king; Act Five, Scene Four: Macbeth ruminates about life's meaning;* and so on. After reading the monologue, invite student groups to discuss and draw symbols representing each image, in sequential order, on a long sheet of paper. Invite each group to read the monologue aloud and slowly unroll 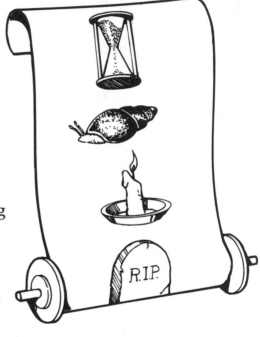 their scroll of pictures, displaying the images as the words are read. Afterward, discuss the monologue with students and which pictures best represent its meaning.

WITCHES ON TRIAL

Have students act out a trial of the three witches. For example, Seyton (the only officer left with Macbeth at the time of his death) takes the three witches to court. Seyton claims the witches should be responsible for Macbeth's actions, but the witches proclaim their innocence. Have groups of five ("Seyton," the three "witches," and a "judge") write scripts and perform their trials for the class. Invite the class to decide which trial was most persuasive in blaming the witches as well as proving their innocence.

MACBETH REVIEW

Show students several examples of newspaper movie reviews and discuss the style in which they are written. Then invite students to write reviews of the play following these directions.

1. Attach a real (or drawn) picture of yourself to a piece of paper, and write your name, grade, and school.

2. Begin your review with one descriptive word such as *boring, exciting,* or *funny.* Write a brief review of the play, including supporting reasons why you chose that particular word.

3. Explain what you believe to be the best and worst aspects of the play.

4. Choose a character you like and one you dislike. Give reasons for your choices and how these characters affected you.

5. Give the play a grade such as: A— *Outstanding,* B—*Good,* C—*Okay,* D—*A bomb!*

SCENE TITLES

Have students write titles for each act and/or scene in the play. For example, Act One, Scene One could be titled *The Witches' Predictions;* and Act Two, Scene One *The Dagger of Duncan's Death.*

RENAISSANCE FEAST

To close your study of the play, celebrate with a Renaissance Feast! Have student groups research the time period (Elizabethan England) in which the play was written via the Internet or the library. Topics can include food, sports and games, clothing, music, entertainment, and so on. Invite each group to share what they learned with the class, and use the information to plan a feast. They can dress up in period clothing, prepare special foods to eat, play games, and listen to period music. You may invite parents and/or another class to your feast so students can share what they learned.

REFERENCES

Calandra, Denis. *Cliffs Notes on Shakespeare's "Macbeth."* Lincoln, Nebraska: Cliffs Notes, Inc., 1979.

Coxwell, Margaret J. "Shakespeare for Elementary Students," *Teaching PreK–8* 27, no. 8 (March 1997): 40–42.

Durband, Alan, ed. *Shakespeare Made Easy: "Macbeth."* New York: Barron's, 1985.

Epstein, Norrie. *The Friendly Shakespeare.* New York: Viking, 1993.

The Illustrated Stratford Shakespeare. London: Chancellor Press, 1982.

Onions, C. T. *A Shakespeare Glossary.* New York: Oxford University Press, 1986.